MANNERS ALL AROUND

by Emma Bassier

Cody Koala

An Imprint of Pop!

popbooksonline.com

abdobooks.com
Published by Pop!, a division of ABDO, PO Box 398166, Minneapolis, Minnesota 55439. Copyright © 2020 by POP, LLC. International copyrights reserved in all countries. No part of this book may be reproduced in any form without written permission from the publisher. Pop!™ is a trademark and logo of POP, LLC.

Printed in the United States of America, North Mankato, Minnesota

102019
012020

THIS BOOK CONTAINS
RECYCLED MATERIALS

Cover Photo: Shutterstock Images
Interior Photos: Shutterstock Images, 1, 7, 21 (top); iStockphoto, 5 (top), 5 (bottom left), 5 (bottom right), 6, 9 (top), 9 (bottom left), 9 (bottom right), 10, 13, 14, 17, 18–19, 21 (bottom left), 21 (bottom right)

Editor: Brienna Rossiter
Series Designer: Jake Slavik

Library of Congress Control Number: 2019942778
Publisher's Cataloging-in-Publication Data
Names: Bassier, Emma, author.
Title: Manners all around / by Emma Bassier
Description: Minneapolis, Minnesota : Pop!, 2020 | Series: Manners matter | Includes online resources and index.
Identifiers: ISBN 9781532165603 (lib. bdg.) | ISBN 9781644942932 (pbk.) | ISBN 9781532166921 (ebook)
Subjects: LCSH: Manners--Juvenile literature. | Polite behavior--Juvenile literature. | Social areas--Juvenile literature. | Social customs--Juvenile literature. | Public places--Juvenile literature.
Classification: DDC 395.12--dc23

Hello! My name is

Cody Koala

Pop open this book and you'll find QR codes like this one, loaded with information, so you can learn even more!

Scan this code* and others like it while you read, or visit the website below to make this book pop.

popbooksonline.com/manners-all-around

*Scanning QR codes requires a web-enabled smart device with a QR code reader app and a camera.

Table of Contents

Chapter 1

Thinking of Others

Manners are the right words and actions for different situations. Words affect how others feel. So do actions. People use manners to show **respect** and care for others.

Watch a video here!

People use manners in
many parts of life. Holding
a door open for someone

shows good manners. So

does letting someone go first

in a line.

Chapter 2

Meeting People

When you meet people, you can use good manners to make them feel welcome. There are many **polite** ways to **greet** others. People may wave, hug, or shake hands.

Learn more here!

When people meet for the first time, they learn one another's names. Using a person's name is polite. So is **pronouncing** the name correctly. If you forget a name, don't be afraid to ask.

In some countries, people greet one another with a kiss on the cheek.

Chapter 3

Tips for Talking

Some manners are for talking. Conversations should go back and forth. Listen when others are talking. Don't **interrupt** or talk over the other person.

Learn more here!

When it's your turn to talk, look at the other person. If someone asks you a question, it is polite to answer. Both of these actions show you are paying attention.

Saying *excuse me* is a polite way to get someone's attention.

Chapter 4

Please and Thank You

Kind words are an important part of showing manners. If you want something, it is **polite** to ask for it instead of taking it.

Complete an
activity here!

If you ask for something,
remember to add the word
please. After someone helps
you, say *thank you*.

Thanking others is polite.
It shows you **appreciate**
what they gave you or what
they did.

If someone thanks you, you can say *you're welcome*. This response shows good manners. The person will feel **respected**. By using manners, people help others feel good.

Use kind words.

Ask to help.

Say thank you.

Making Connections

Text-to-Self

Think of a time someone said *please* or *thank you* to you. Where were you? How did it make you feel?

Text-to-Text

Have you read other books about manners? How were those books similar to or different from this book?

Text-to-World

People around the world have different ways of greeting one another. What is a polite way to greet people where you live?

Glossary

appreciate – to notice and be happy about something.

greet – to say hello.

interrupt – to start talking while someone else is still talking.

polite – showing good manners.

pronounce – to say a word or name the correct way.

respect – a way of treating others that shows you care about their thoughts and feelings.

Index

Online Resources

popbooksonline.com

Thanks for reading this Cody Koala book!

Scan this code* and others like it in this book, or visit the website below to make this book pop!

popbooksonline.com/manners-all-around

*Scanning QR codes requires a web-enabled smart device with a QR code reader app and a camera.